WORLD: Surfing

Paul Mason

Th
ab
tele

Produced for A & C Black by
Monkey Puzzle Media Ltd
11 Chanctonbury Road
Hove BN3 6EL, UK

Published by A & C Black, an imprint
of Bloomsbury Publishing Plc
50 Bedford Square
London WC1B 3DP

www.acblack.com
www.bloomsbury.com

First published in paperback 2012
Copyright © 2012 Bloomsbury
Publishing Plc

ISBN 978-1-4081-4032-1

A CIP catalogue record for this book is
available from the British Library.

Editor: Dan Rogers
Design: Mayer Media
Picture research: Lynda Lines

This book is produced using paper that
is made from wood grown in managed,
sustainable forests. It is natural,
renewable and recyclable. The logging
and manufacturing processes conform
to the environmental regulations of the
country of origin.

Printed and bound in China by
C&C Offset Printing Co.

1 3 5 7 9 10 8 6 4 2

Picture acknowledgements
Action Images pp. 13 (Benjamin
Thouard/DPPI), 20–21 (Kelly Cestari/
Zuma Press), 21 top (Reuters), 26; Alamy
pp. 5 (Imagebroker), 8 (James Davis
Photography), 12 (Hemis), 14 (Ultimate
Group, LLC), 16 (Lonely Planet Images),
24–25 (Photo Resource Hawaii); ASP
p. 10–11; Bluegreen Pictures p. 9 (Barry
Bland); Corbis pp. 1 Hugh Gentry/
Reuters), 11 top (Gene Blevins), 19 top
(Sylvain Cazenave), 25 top (Hugh Gentry/
Reuters); Lucia Griggi/UKPSA p. 22 left;
iStockphoto p. 7; MPM Images pp. 6–7,
17 bottom, 28–29; PA Photos p. 27 (Ben
Margot/AP); Photolibrary pp. 4 (JTB
Photo), 15 (Vince Cavataro/Pacific Stock),
17 top (Chris Laurens), 18–19 (Tom
Servais/Monsoon Images), 29 top (Ron
Dahlquist/Pacific Stock); Matt Smith
p. 22 right; surf.co.nz p. 23.
Compass rose artwork on front cover
and inside pages by iStockphoto. Map
artwork by MPM Images.

The front cover shows Heitor Alves
competing in the Santa Catarina Pro,
part of the ASP World Tour (Action
Images/Kirstin Scholtz/ASP).

Every effort has been made to
contact copyright holders of material
reproduced in this book. Any omissions
will be rectified in subsequent printings
if notice is given to the publishers.

SAFETY ADVICE

Don't attempt any of the
activities or techniques
in this book without the
guidance of a qualified
instructor.

CONTENTS

It's a Surf-tastic World

As the wave swells behind you, you paddle hard for the beach. The board slides down the wave face and you leap smoothly to your feet. You crouch down to make yourself small. The wave curls over you and suddenly you're screaming along inside a spiralling tube of water. Sound good? Welcome to the world of surfing.

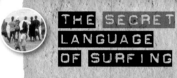

THE SECRET LANGUAGE OF SURFING

locals people who often surf at a place
rash vest thin nylon T-shirt

THE WORLD OF SURFING

To become a surfer, you need to know words from the secret language of surfing, such as "left-hander", "reef break" and "hold-down". You also need to know what equipment the **locals** use in different conditions, where to go for the best waves, and how to behave and keep safe out in the water. And – of course – how to surf.

No need for a wetsuit for these surfers, about to hit the warm waves off Hawaii.

Technical: Renting surfing equipment

When you first start surfing, it's usually best to rent equipment, rather than buying it.

Board:

• Most beginners learn on either longboards, which are at least 2.6 metres (8 feet 6 inches) long or funboards, usually 2.15 to 2.6 metres (7 feet to 8 feet 6 inches).

• More experienced surfers usually ride shorter boards.

Wetsuit:

• In warm water, surf shorts and a **rash vest** or wetsuit top are enough.

• In colder conditions, a full wetsuit, and even boots and gloves, might be needed.

Other equipment:

• A leash attaches the board to your ankle, stopping it being swept to the beach when you fall off.

• Wax is rubbed on to the board to help your feet grip.

A very determined surfer somewhere close to the Arctic Circle! Modern surf gear means even the coldest water is open to surf explorers.

PASSPORT TO SURFING

Fortunately, all the information you need is in this book – which is your passport to surfing around the world.

Do you want to become a great surfer? And if you could travel the whole world to learn, where would be the best places to visit? Turn the page (and keep turning!) to find out more...

Freshwater Beach

Australia is one of the world's best surfing countries. Where better to start your global surf journey than the beach where Australian surfing began? Freshwater is where Hawaii's Duke Kahanamoku first demonstrated surfing to Australians in 1915.

SURFING FRESHWATER

Freshwater is a sandy beach at the edge of the city of Sydney. The surf can get crowded, so (like everywhere!) remember the drop-in rule:

If someone else is already riding the wave, or is closer to the curl than you, you mustn't catch it.

Apart from that, the sandy bottom and gentle waves make this a great spot to start surfing.

FRESHWATER BEACH
Location: New South Wales, Australia
Type of surf: beach break
Difficulty level: 1.5 of 5
Best season: November to March

Tip from a Local
Even on cloudy days, put on sunscreen – the sun here is very strong!

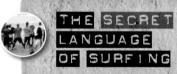

THE SECRET LANGUAGE OF SURFING

nose front 30 centimetres (12 inches) of a surfboard

wax up rub wax on the top of a surfboard

Swell pours into the beach at Freshwater, NSW – the spot where surfing first came ashore in Australia.

SKILL
Getting out through the waves

The first challenge for anyone learning to surf is paddling the board out through the breaking waves.

1. Walk out, pushing the board along beside you, until the water is chest deep. NEVER have the board in front of you – waves will whack it back at you.

2. Lie on the board facing forwards. Aim to balance so that the **nose** of the board is about 10 centimetres (4 inches) above the water level. This is how the board will paddle best.

3. Paddle out using long, deep, steady strokes, as if you were doing front crawl.

4. If a wave is about to push you backwards, "turn turtle". Turn the board over so you are underneath it, and hold on to the sides to stop it being dragged away.

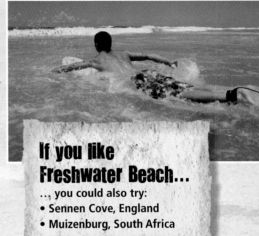

Just two lines of white water ahead – probably a pretty easy paddle out for this surfer.

If you like Freshwater Beach...

.., you could also try:
• Sennen Cove, England
• Muizenburg, South Africa

ESSENTIAL INFORMATION

Freshwater is best for beginners in the summer, from November to March. In winter, bigger waves roll in and that's when the experts **wax up** their boards.

Surfboard: People ride all kinds of boards at Freshwater, but a funboard of about 2.3 metres (7 feet 6 inches) is best for beginner surfers.

Wetsuit: Rarely needed, except a top to keep off the sun.

Hazards: In summer, little bluebottle jellyfish can give you a nasty sting, though they aren't deadly. Attacks by great white sharks have also happened along this coast.

Saunton Sands

At Saunton Sands, you don't have to look far for traditional English seaside sights. Hats made of newspaper, ice-cream cones, and large areas of sunburned flesh are all on display. But the beach will also be piled high with surfboards – this is one of the most popular surf spots in England.

SAUNTON SANDS
Location: Devon, England
Type of surf: beach break
Difficulty level: 1.5 of 5
Best season: May to July and September

If you like Saunton Sands...

... you could also try:
- Tullan Strand, Ireland
- Costa da Caparica, Portugal

SURFING SAUNTON SANDS

Because of their popularity, the waves at Saunton sometimes get very crowded. If they are, don't worry – the beach is 5 kilometres (3.1 miles) long! All you need to do is walk for 10 minutes, and you'll be able to surf alone. In winter, the surf gets much bigger and breaks a long way from shore – not very good for beginners.

Saunton is such a big beach that even if it's busy, there's room for everyone.

ESSENTIAL INFORMATION

During summer, Saunton usually has small, peeling waves that are perfect for beginners.

Surfboard: Most people ride big longboards, of 2.9 metres (9 feet 6 inches) or more. This helps you to catch the waves, which are not very powerful.

Wetsuit: A wetsuit is needed all year round, but in summer a **3/2** wetsuit is enough.

Hazards: Weever fish can give your feet a nasty sting if you tread on them.

Tip from a Local
Don't plan a special trip to Saunton in August – the surf is often flat!

SKILL
catching waves

Once you've got the board out to where the waves are breaking, the next step is to turn it around and catch a wave back to the beach.

1. Sit up on the board, as if you were on a horse. Balance so that the nose is pointing upwards.

2. When you see a wave coming, spin the board round (this is easier with its nose still pointing up).

3. Lie on the board as you did when paddling out, and start paddling in towards the shore as fast as possible.

4. Aim to paddle the board only a little slower than the wave is moving. If you manage this, the wave will start to push the board towards the beach. You're surfing!

THE SECRET LANGUAGE OF SURFING

3/2 wetsuit made of both 3 millimetre and 2 millimetre (0.12 and 0.08 inch) thick material

Paddling for a tubing wave – the surfer on the left is going to catch this one.

The ASP World Tour

If you want to see some of the world's biggest **rippers**, check out the ASP World Tour. This is a contest for the world's top competitive surfers. There are separate versions for men and women, but sometimes the men's and women's contests are held in the same place.

THE SECRET LANGUAGE OF SURFING

ripper fast, aggressive surfer

THE BEST SURFERS, ON THE BEST WAVES

The Tour lasts nearly the whole year, with contests in Europe, North America, Australia and the Pacific. In each area, the organizers pick the best surf spots. In some places, such as south-west France, they even wait to decide where the contest will be held until they know exactly where conditions will be best.

THE ASP WORLD TOUR
Location: worldwide
Type of surf: all types
Difficulty level: 5 of 5
Best season: February to December

MEN: ●
1. *February–March* Gold Coast, Australia
2. *March–April* Bell's Beach, Australia
3. *April–May* Santa Catarina, Brazil
4. *July* Jeffrey's Bay, South Africa
5. *August–September* Teahupoo, French Polynesia
6. *September* Trestles, California, USA
7. *September–October* south-west France
8. *October* Peniche, Portugal
9. *November* Isabela, Puerto Rico
10. *December* Pipeline, Hawaii, USA

WOMEN:
1. *February–March* Gold Coast, Australia
2. *March–April* Bell's Beach, Australia
3. *April* Taranaki, New Zealand
4. *April* Dee Why Beach, Australia
5. *June* San Bartolo, Peru
6. *October* Peniche, Portugal
7. *November* Isabela, Puerto Rico
8. *November–December* Sunset Beach, Hawaii, USA

ASP WORLD CHAMPION

Over the course of the year, surfers win points depending on where they come in the individual events. At the end of the year, whoever has the most points is the World Champion. The most successful surfer ever is Kelly Slater – who has been World Champion an amazing TEN times. No other surfer has won the championship more than four times.

Kelly Slater, ten times World Surfing Champion, ripping in a contest at Trestles, USA.

Visit an ASP contest like this one at Bell's Beach, Australia, and you'll see some of the world's best surfers. They surf even better live than they do on DVD!

Kuta Beach

Every surfer aims to visit Bali one day. The island is famous for being a friendly, relaxed place, which fits perfectly with the surfing **vibe**. And nothing beats walking barefoot to the beach – especially when you get there and see that the waves are **going off**!

KUTA BEACH
Location: Bali, Indonesia
Type of surf: beach break
Difficulty level: 2 of 5
Best season: November to March

SURFING KUTA

Bali is home to some of the world's most famous surf breaks – but these are for experts only! They break in shallow water, over sharp reefs. Fortunately, Kuta Beach is great for beginners. In summer the waves are usually small – good for practising! And the sea has a sandy bottom, so when you do fall off, it rarely hurts.

THE SECRET LANGUAGE OF SURFING

vibe feeling or atmosphere
going off really good

If you don't bring a board (or the airline breaks it!), don't worry – you can rent one from the cat in the hat.

12

Tip from a Local

Look out for the baskets of flowers and incense left on the ground – they are offerings to Bali's Hindu gods.

SKILL
Standing up

Sometimes, you don't even need to get to your feet to have a blast on a surfboard! This rider is halfway up, and already having a great time.

ESSENTIAL INFORMATION

Kuta is best for beginners during the summer, making it a great place for a Christmas surfing holiday!

Surfboard: A longboard is probably best for learning to catch waves at Kuta. The extra length will help you catch the waves, which sometimes break quickly, earlier.

Wetsuit: Not needed; board shorts and rash vest to keep off the sun.

Hazards: One of the beach sellers might persuade you to buy an unsuitable flowery shirt.

If you like Kuta Beach...

… you could also try:
- Bondi Beach, Australia
- Waikiki Beach, Hawaii, USA
- Pointe de la Torche, France

Standing up on a surfboard is probably the single hardest thing to learn. Maybe that's why the moment when you first manage it lives in your memory forever!

1. Once the surfboard has started to slide forwards, push up with your arms into a press-up position.

2. Slide your legs forwards so that you are on one knee. (If you are more comfortable with your left leg forwards, you're a "natural-footer". If it's your right leg, you're a "goofy footer".)

3. Once you feel balanced, stand up into a crouch. Aim to have your feet across the centre line of the board, and your body sideways. Your head and shoulders twist forwards so that you can see where you're going!

13

San Onofre

There is said to have been a surf camp at San Onofre since the 1920s, and it is one of the birthplaces of Californian surfing. San Onofre is really several different surf spots all collected in one area. The key **breaks** are increasingly oddly named: The Point, Old Man's and Dogpatch.

SAN ONOFRE
Location: California, USA
Type of surf: beach and reef breaks
Difficulty level: 2.5 of 5
Best season: all year round

THE SECRET LANGUAGE OF SURFING

break surf spot
in trim gliding smoothly along a wave

SURFING SAN ONOFRE

For practising your technique, a long ride is ideal – and San Onofre is famous as a place where surfers can get rides of 300 to 500 metres (about 985 to 1640 feet)! The waves start breaking at less than waist-high, but they can get much bigger. Waves bigger than chest-high are probably not suitable for improver surfers.

A beautiful beach day (which to be fair isn't that unusual in Southern California) and a nice little swell – a perfect day for surfing "San-O".

Tip from a Local
If you can, go to San Onofre on a weekday – there will be fewer surfers in the water, so you'll catch more waves.

SKILL
Trimming the board

Trimming the board means keeping it gliding along the wave, instead of heading straight into the beach:

If you like San Onofre...
... you could also try:
- Jan Juc, Australia
- Banana Beach, Morocco

ESSENTIAL INFORMATION
It can be a long walk to the breaks at San Onofre, so make sure you are comfortable carrying your board. It will seem a lot heavier on the walk back from the beach!

Surfboard: Either a funboard or a longboard is ideal in this area.

Wetsuit: May not be needed during summer, but in winter surfers definitely need some protection from the cold.

Hazards: Great white sharks have been spotted in the water, though attacks are rare.

Trimming across the face of the wave, matching the speed at which it's breaking.

1. Try to catch the wave with the board pointing slightly sideways. An angle of about 45 degrees to the wave is about right.

2. The board will automatically slide along the wave as you stand up. Now you need to keep it **in trim**.

3. To rise up the face of the wave, put a little extra weight on to your back foot. To drop down (and pick up speed), put a little weight on your front foot.

4. Practise rising and falling to get a feel for how to steer the board along the wave.

Raglan

The island country of New Zealand lies far out in the Pacific Ocean. Surrounded by deep ocean, the islands always have somewhere worth surfing. But the place most of the world's surfers dream of one day riding is the left-hand **point breaks** of Raglan.

In the right conditions, the left-handers on the point at Raglan are among the world's longest waves.

Tip from a Local

Check out the first-ever film of Raglan, in the classic 1966 surf movie *Endless Summer*.

RAGLAN
Location: North Island, New Zealand
Type of surf: beach, reef and point breaks
Difficulty level: 3 of 5
Best season: April to September

SURFING RAGLAN

Raglan is actually made up of five different surf breaks: three point breaks, a reef break and a beach break. The point breaks sometimes connect, making it possible to ride one wave for over 3 kilometres (1.9 miles)! On these days, the surfers finish their rides, get out of the water, and get a lift back to the start of the wave in a car.

If you like Raglan...
... you could also try:
- Ribeira d'Ilhas, Portugal
- Chicama, Peru

SKILL
Turning the board

THE SECRET LANGUAGE OF SURFING

point break wave that breaks along a piece of land sticking out into the ocean

ESSENTIAL INFORMATION

The best wave for improvers is Manu Point, which is usually smaller than the other two point breaks.

Surfboard: You can ride any board at Raglan, but most people ride funboards or shortboards.

Wetsuit: A wetsuit is needed, as the water when the surf is best will be about 15° Centigrade (59° Fahrenheit).

Hazards: Great whites have attacked several people in the area over the years.

Top turns get you speed on small waves in just the same way as on big ones.

On a wave as long as Raglan, just trimming along in a straight line would get very boring. You need to learn to turn!

1. Always keep your knees bent when doing turns. Turns going in the direction your toes point are called forehand turns. Going the other way is called backhand.

2. Turns up the wave are done by putting extra weight on your back foot, and leaning the board over like you would a skateboard or snowboard.

3. To turn down the wave, lean forwards to put extra weight on your front foot. Again, lean the board over – having bent knees will help you to do this.

Carissa Moore of Hawaii sets up a BIG bottom turn. Surfing waves this powerful takes a lot of skill and commitment.

17

The Triple Crown

Ah, Hawaii – where the air and sea temperatures stay at about 26° Centigrade (79° Fahrenheit) all year round, and the beaches are home to some of the best waves in the world. It's a surfer's paradise! No wonder the Triple Crown, one of the biggest events of the surfing year, is held here.

THE TRIPLE CROWN
Location: Oahu, Hawaii, USA
Type of surf: beach, reef and point breaks
Difficulty level: 5 of 5
Held: November and December

CLIMAX OF THE SURFING YEAR

The Triple Crown brings the competitive surfing year to a finish. The contest is made up of three surfing events, all held on the North Shore of Oahu:
• the Pipeline Masters, at Pipeline
• the Hawaiian Pro, at Haleiwa
• the World Cup, at Sunset Beach.
These three breaks are among the world's most famous – and most dangerous – surf spots.

THE PIPELINE MASTERS

The contest at Pipeline is probably the one contest that surfers would most like to win. The wave is a fast-moving, twisting barrel of water. It breaks over a **reef bottom** that's filled with cracks and caves, in which several surfers have been trapped and drowned. Even to catch a wave here you have to be one of the world's best surfers. To win a contest takes something very special.

Tip from a Local

If you're going to see a Triple Crown contest, take some binoculars – they make watching a lot more exciting!

The waves at Sunset Beach are sometimes said to be the toughest test anywhere of a surfer's all-round ability.

Spectators look on as a competitor drops into a big one on a windy day at Pipeline.

THE SECRET LANGUAGE OF SURFING

reef bottom seabed made of coral reef

rbank

SUPERBANK
Location: Queensland, Australia
Type of surf: point break
Difficulty level: 4 of 5
Best season: December to
March and May to August

It's no accident that several world champion surfers have come from Queensland. This area is so good for surfing that there's even a city here called Surfer's Paradise. All up and down the coast are brilliant breaks, the sun seems to shine all the time and the water is usually warm.

SURFING SUPERBANK
Superbank's overriding feature is the speed at which the wave breaks. Surfers can travel the 1.5 kilometres (0.9 miles) from the point at Snapper Rocks to the beach at lightning speed – if they're good enough! Slower-moving board riders will be quickly **wiped out** by the foaming white water.

ESSENTIAL INFORMATION
Smaller waves are most likely from December to March. Bigger waves, which are really for expert surfers, usually happen between May and August.

Surfboard: A shortboard or, in smaller surf, a **fish** are good boards for Superbank.

Wetsuit: Not needed.

Hazards: The biggest danger is that you won't catch any waves! This is a very, very crowded break. Also, watch out for sharks.

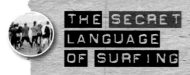

If you like Superbank...
... you could also try:
- Mundaka, Spain
- Trestles, California, USA

THE SECRET LANGUAGE OF SURFING
wipe out fall off your surfboard
fish short, wide-tailed board with two fins

Tip from a Local
After riding a wave, most people get out of the sea and walk back up the point, instead of paddling.

SKILL
Surfing faster

Surfing faster makes it possible to increase the fun you get from a wave. You can make more turns and generally get extra excitement from each ride.

1. Keep your knees bent, and lean your weight forwards. You should be aiming for your chest to be over your front foot.

2. Pick up speed by dropping down the face and turning back up it. Little turns, snaking along the wave, are sometimes called "pumping" the board for speed.

3. Use your hips and knees to keep the board snaking along. You can practise

Hawaii's Sunny Garcia screaming out of the tube, in trim for speed — his weight is forwards on the board, over his front foot.

this movement on a skateboard: push off, and try to keep the board moving for as long as possible with the movement of your hips.

Kelly Slater tucks into a ridiculously small barrel at Superbank.

Thurso Reef

Say "dream surf trip" to most people, and they think of palm trees, warm water and sunny days. Thurso offers a dream surf trip with a difference: wind-blasted trees, freezing water and a lot of rain. It might sound like a nightmare – but it isn't!

THURSO REEF
Location: Caithness, Scotland
Type of surf: reef break
Difficulty level: 4.5 of 5
Best season: October to April

SURFING THURSO

Surfers come to Thurso from all over the world for one reason: the waves. The power and shape of the waves rank with the best in the world, yet they are rarely crowded. This is one of the few places in the world where you can surf great waves for hours, with just a few other people in the line-up.

Tip from a Local

Don't worry about the brown water – it's coloured by peat that has washed down Thurso River, and is harmless.

ESSENTIAL INFORMATION

Surfboard: Bigger, narrower boards work well here, for example a 2.3-metre (7 foot 6 inch) **gun**.

Wetsuit: Definitely! The water here is cold, even in summer. In winter, you need a winter suit, boots, gloves and a hat – and you still won't be able to stay in for more than 45 minutes.

Hazards: In winter, freezing to death. In summer, being driven mad by biting insects.

After winning a contest at Thurso, pro surfer Micah Lester said it was, "The best right-hander in the country, and maybe in Europe."

Peaty water adds atmosphere to this Thurso tube. On a small day like this, the reef can be surfed by improvers, but when it's big, it's for experts only!

Blair Stewart, set up for a beautiful tube ride, somewhere in the Pacific.

Tube riding is one of the trickiest surfing manoeuvres. It is made harder because waves only tube over a shallow bottom – if you fall off, it often hurts!

1. A fast take-off is crucial. Paddle hard, and as soon as the board catches the wave, leap to your feet.

2. Turn hard off the bottom of the wave and then straighten out to ride along it.

3. Try to judge where the wave will throw a lip out, creating a tube. If you are approaching this section too fast, you may need to **stall** the board by weighting the tail and lifting the nose up.

4. Crouch down small, and ride through the tube. To slow down inside it, drag your hand through the wave face.

If you like Thurso Reef...

... you could also try:
• Shoals Reef, Alaska, USA
• Firlikhy, Norway

THE SECRET LANGUAGE OF SURFING

gun narrow surfboard designed for powerful waves

stall slow down or stop moving

23

The Eddie

The Eddie is the jewel in the crown of big-wave surfing contests. It is named after Eddie Aikau, who was a lifeguard at Waimea Bay in Hawaii. Eddie regularly saved swimmers and surfers from the bay's giant surf. After he died, the contest was set up in his memory.

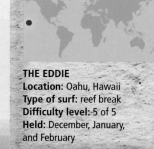

THE EDDIE
Location: Oahu, Hawaii
Type of surf: reef break
Difficulty level: 5 of 5
Held: December, January, and February

Waimea as seen from the hills behind the Bay, on a good 6 metre plus (20 foot) day.

THE BAY CALLS THE DAY

Some years, the Eddie doesn't get held. That's because it only happens when the mid-winter surf in Waimea Bay is bigger than 6.1 metres (20 feet). This means the **wave faces** will be more like 9 metres (almost 30 feet)! Smaller waves are not enough of a challenge for the big-wave riders who take part in the Eddie.

A photographer and a rescue crew look on as a competitor drops into a straight-hander at the Eddie.

AN INVITATION-ONLY PARTY

You can't just post off an entry form and take part in the Eddie. You have to be invited. The contest organizers invite 28 of the world's best big-wave surfers to take part. They also ask several other surfers to act as "alternates", who will get an entry if any of the 28 drop out.

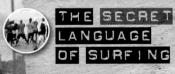

THE SECRET LANGUAGE OF SURFING

wave face front slope of a wave

Tip from a Local

In "smaller" surf, Waimea Bay has waves that break off its rocky side – the only trouble is, "small" here still means taller than a grown man!

Maverick's

ESSENTIAL INFORMATION

Surfboard: BIG! A long, slim board over 2.75 metres (9 feet).

Wetsuit: The northern California water is cold, so a full winter wetsuit, plus gloves, hat and boots, are needed.

Hazards: The waves themselves are killers; you might get washed into the jagged rocks on shore; and there are plenty of great white sharks around.

It's hard to imagine a more frightening place to surf than Maverick's. The water is cold, the wave breaks far out to sea and the sky often seems overcast and gloomy. To cap it all off, the break is inside the Red Triangle – an area of ocean off northern California where shark attacks are common.

SURFING MAVERICK'S

This fearsome wave only starts to break when the surf is about 3 metres (nearly 10 feet) high! Waves up to 12 metres (almost 40 feet) high have been surfed here. For years, local surfer Jeff Clark surfed Maverick's alone – starting when he was just 18 years old! After 15 years, Clark got bored and told a few friends about his surf spot, and Maverick's quickly became world-famous.

Spectators line the cliffs during a big-wave session at Maverick's. Competition or not, this place always draws a crowd.

Tip from a Local
The best place to watch the surfers at Maverick's is from the cliffs at Pillar Point.

If you like Maverick's...
... you could also try:
• **Dungeons, South Africa**
• **Todos Santos, Mexico**

SKILL
Riding Giants

Surfing giant waves like those at Maverick's takes special skills and equipment.

• The surfers ride **rhino chasers**: long boards, over 2.75 metres (9 feet), but with narrow, spear-like shapes. The length helps them catch the giant waves. The narrow nose stops the board being blown back up the face of the wave as the surfer paddles. The pointed tail helps the board grip the wave face once the surfer has stood up.

• Catching big waves takes tremendous paddling speed, so the surfers have to be very fit. They also have to be able to hold their breath for over a minute at a time – that's how long a big wave can hold you underwater if you wipe out. And a big-wave rider must stay calm in situations where ordinary people would panic.

What if you jumped off a cliff, then the cliff jumped on top of you? This is definitely going to hurt.

THE SECRET LANGUAGE OF SURFING

rhino chaser surfboard for riding big waves

Teahupoo

First, pronunciation: it's pronounced "Cho-pu". Get that wrong, and you will never live it down! Teahupoo is a mutant wave – incredibly powerful and thicker than it is high. It breaks over a shallow reef, far from the shore. All in all, this one is definitely for expert surfers only.

TEAHUPOO
Location: Tahiti, French Polynesia
Type of surf: reef break
Difficulty level: 5 of 5
Best season: May to December

If you like Teahupoo...

… you could also try:
- **Shipstern Bluff, Australia**
- **Ghost Trees, California, USA**

SURFING TEAHUPOO

The wave at Teahupoo breaks and peels very quickly, throwing out a thick lip of water. Recently, surfers have started to use tow-in techniques to ride the biggest waves. They are towed into the path of the wave behind a jet ski. This builds up enough speed for them to catch the wave earlier, and get longer tube rides.

ESSENTIAL INFORMATION

Surfboard: For traditional paddle surfing, a 2- to 2.3-metre- (6 foot 6 inch to 7 foot 6 inch) board. Tow-in surfers use specialist boards (see Skill panel).

Wetsuit: Not needed in the warm water.

Hazards: Shallow reef; the possible embarrassment of getting there and finding you're too scared to catch a wave.

Tip from a Local
Don't go out unless you're SURE you are good enough – at least one experienced local surfer has been killed at Teahupoo.

How scary is that? A crowd of surfers watches Teahupoo at its best/worst. Anyone who says he's not a little bit nervous is about to grow an extra-long nose, like Pinocchio when he lied.

THE SECRET LANGUAGE OF SURFING

chop small peaks on the surface of the water

SKILL
Tow-in surfing

You can just about see the tow line in this photo – it's the yellow thing bouncing in the jet ski's wake.

In the twenty-first century, tow-in surfing has become an increasingly popular way of catching waves that are simply too big to be caught in a traditional way.

• The surfers use specially designed boards. They are short but heavy, to help them cut through the **chop** on the faces of big waves. The boards also have footstraps to hold the surfer's feet firmly in place.

• The surfer is towed up to speed behind a jet ski, holding on to a rope. Once in position on the wave, the surfer drops the rope.

• Surfers often wear buoyancy aids, to stop them being held under the surface for too long if they wipe out.

Glossary

Words from the Secret Language features

3/2 wetsuit made of both 3 millimetre and 2 millimetre (0.12 and 0.08 inch) thick material. A 3/2 is often called a "summer suit". In winter, surfers wear 5/3s – 5 millimetres (0.2 inches) thick on the body and 3 millimetres (0.12 inches) thick on the arms.

break surf spot

chop small peaks on the water surface, usually caused by wind

fish short, wide-tailed board with two fins

going off really good, used to describe both waves and surfers

gun narrow surfboard, designed for powerful waves. A typical gun is 2.15 to 2.45 metres (7 to 8 feet) long, thick, and with a narrow nose and tail.

in trim gliding smoothly along a wave

locals people who often surf a place. Many locals are friendly but in some crowded spots they try to discourage other surfers from joining in. This is called localism.

nose front 30 centimetres (12 inches) of a surfboard

point break wave that breaks along a piece of land sticking out into the ocean

rash vest thin nylon T-shirt, used to stop your wetsuit rubbing against your skin and giving you a rash. Some rash vests can also be used to protect your skin from the sun's rays.

reef bottom seabed made of coral reef

rhino chaser surfboard for riding big waves, usually over 2.75 metres (9 feet) long and with a narrow nose and tail

ripper fast, aggressive surfer; rippers are typically also "going off" (see above)

stall slow down or stop moving

vibe feeling or atmosphere, a former hippy term that was originally short for "vibration"

wave face front slope of a wave, along which a surfer rides

wax up rub wax on the top of a surfboard. Once done, this is sometimes called a "wax job".

wipe out fall off your surfboard

Other words surfers use

beach break wave that breaks close to a beach. The bottom may be sandy, rocky or a mixture of the two.

malibu another name for a longboard

mini-mal another name for a funboard

rail thin edge of a surfboard

reef break wave that breaks over a reef, a raised area of the seabed

tail back 30 centimetres (12 inches) of a surfboard

Finding Out More

THE INTERNET

www.wannasurf.com
This is one of the best surf-travel related websites. You can find local information on just about any surf spot in the world. Narrow down your search by continent, country, region and location.

www.magicseaweed.com
This is a useful site for travelling surfers. It uses information from wave buoys around the world to generate forecasts for how big and how good the surf will be at thousands of beaches.

BOOKS

Though none of the following are specifically aimed at young readers, they are easy to read and would be suitable for anyone able to read alone with confidence:

The World Stormrider Guide Antony Colas and Bruce Sutherland (Low Pressure, latest edition 2009)
This book picks out highlights from the world surfing scene, and gives advice about water temperature, what kind of wetsuit you might need, typical wave size and general travel information.

Surfing the World Chris Nelson and Demi Taylor (Footprint, latest edition 2008)
This brilliantly researched book is full of information about hundreds of European and Moroccan surf spots. Part of a series by the same authors, which also includes *Surfing Britain and Ireland* and *Surfing Europe*.

Surfing Australia Mark Thornley and Veda Dante (Periplus, 1999)
Though old, this is still available and remains one of the best guides to surfing in Australia. It is part of a series of books that also includes *Surfing Hawaii* and *Surfing Indonesia*.

MAGAZINES

Most surf magazines carry a mixture of articles on equipment, personalities, contests and travel. They all have websites you can locate by searching by name.

Surfer and *Surfing*
These are the two biggest surf magazines, found in surf shops and newsagents around the world. Both are US-based and largely focused on surfing in the USA.

Surfer's Path
This British magazine is also published in the USA. It focuses on the European and US surf scenes.

Tracks and *Australia's Surfing Life* (known as *ASL*)
These Australian magazines both cover surfing from an Australian viewpoint.

Index